A WORKBOOK

The Water Age

Children's Art and Writing Workshops

Tracey Warr

MEANDA BOOKS

Meanda Books
https://meandabooks.com

Cover by James A. Hudson.

Book Layout © 2017 BookDesignTemplates.com

The Water Age #3: Children's Art and Writing Workshops/ Tracey Warr. -- 1st ed.
ISBN 978-0-9954902-5-3

For my sister, Julie

The Water Age Series

The Water Age and Other Fictions (#1)
The Water Age Art and Writing Workshops (#2)
The Water Age Children's Art and Writing Workshops (#3)

The Water Age is a series of three books by Tracey Warr. The books contemplate water and futures through fiction and through art and writing workshops. The books were produced as part of the *Frontiers in Retreat* project. They were co-produced by HIAP, with the support of the EU Culture Programme.

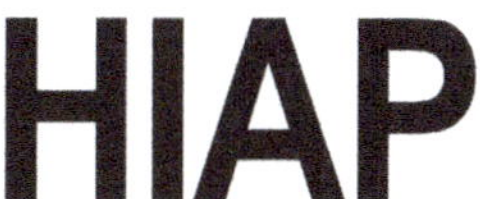 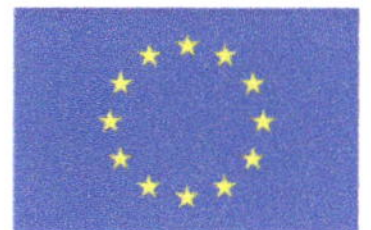

This project has been funded with support from the European Commission. This publication reflects the views only of the author, and the Commission cannot be held responsible for any use which may be made of the information contained therein.

CONTENTS

{ 1 }

Introduction

These workshops focus on the topic of water and are aimed at children in the 8–11 age range. The workshops can be adapted to take place over one afternoon or over a number of sessions and a number of weeks. If you have enough time, it would also be possible to combine the art and writing workshop exercises. Breaks and specific timings can be built into the activities. They can be undertaken with a resident artist or writer or with the class teacher or workshop leader. The Resources for Further Study section lists a selection of relevant books and websites for children and for teachers, which can be used in conjunction with these exercises.

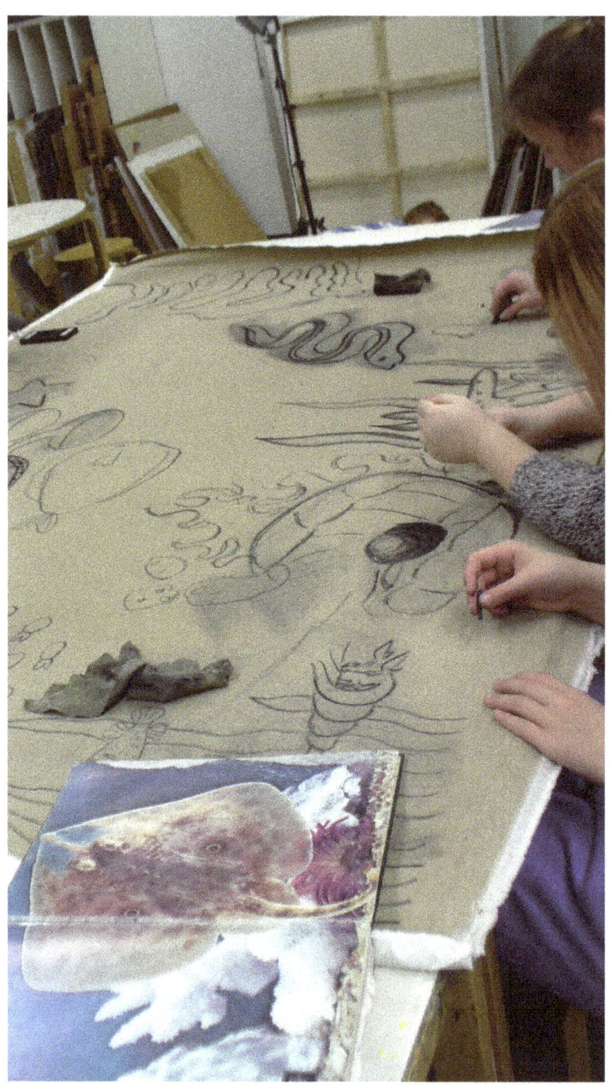

Tracey Warr, Children's Water Art Workshop, Annantalo Art School, Helsinki, Finland, 2015. Part of *Frontiers in Retreat*. Photo by Tracey Warr.

{ 2 }

Topic—The Water Age

Water Facts

Some water facts to share with the group of participants:

The water you drink has been through the bladder of a Tyranno-saurus rex and many other places.

The water on Earth recycles through the water cycle, falling to the ground as rain, hail, sleet and snow; forming ice, dew and puddles; soaking through the ground to aquifers (underground water reservoirs in rocks) or travelling in rivers to the sea; evaporating back into the atmosphere as mist, fog and clouds. Water spends an average of nine days in the sky before falling again. Some water is also stored deep in the Earth's core in serpentine rock and seeps out through cracks in the ocean floor or bursts out through geysers or volcanic eruptions.

The water on Earth is around 4.4 billion years old. Some scientists have suggested that water travelled here through space from a giant 'space spring' in the Milky Way where oxygen and hydrogen are collided together.

Water is essential to humans and all life on the planet. Water has three states: liquid, gas and solid.

The oceans cover 71% of the world's surface. Only 2.5% of the world's water is freshwater rather than saltwater. Around 67% of the human body is water.

In addition to drinking water, watering plants and fishing in water, we also use water for washing, cooking, transport, leisure, in industry and to generate electricity.

Discuss how you feel about water and being in water? Do you love it, or fear it?

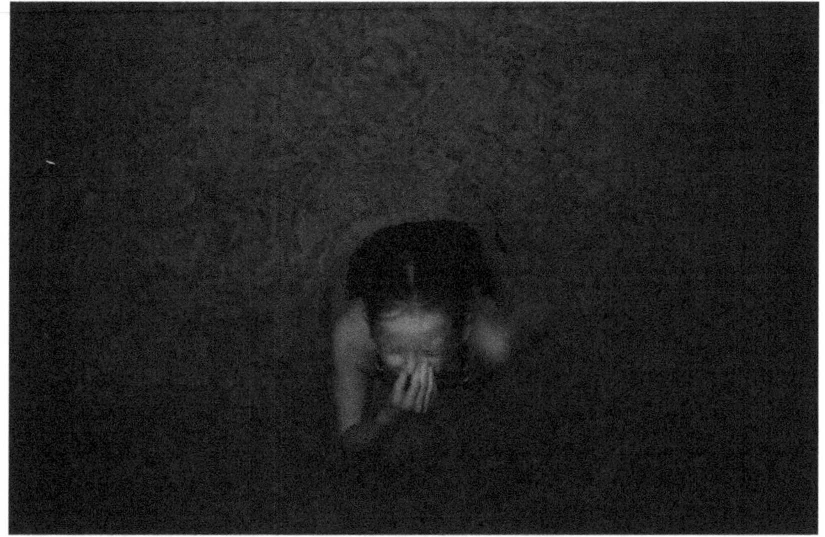

Swimmer. Photo by James A. Hudson.

Future Water

The brief for the workshops:

We may be living with more water in the future. With global warming, sea water is getting warmer and therefore expanding, more rain is falling in some places, ice caps are melting and the water on the planet needs more room. The consequences of global warming are rising sea levels in some parts of the world. In particular, low-lying islands and coastal settlements are likely to be affected by winter storm surges, extreme weather events and flooding. Many parts of the world have already had to cope with major flooding. If all the ice caps were to melt, the UK would become more like an archipelago—a group of many small islands.

In the past, people have found ways to protect the land from the water with dykes, flood barriers and other forms of water engineering, but, in the future, we may have to accept that water needs more room and we will be living with more water. The following workshop exercises look at positive approaches to living in a possible future Water Age.

Aquatic Flora and Fauna

If we were trying to live with more water in the future, could we learn some useful lessons from aquatic lifeforms that live in, on or near water, including fish; marine mammals such as dolphins, whales, otters and seals; aquatic plants; amphibians such as frogs; aquatic insects; molluscs such as mussels and cockles; and water birds? Biomimicry, or copying how animals and other lifeforms work, is a well-established method used in human architecture and design.

Ask the class to look up information on how aquatic creatures and plants cope with their water environments. Sea otters, for example, have long tails to balance them when swimming or sleeping. They often 'hold hands' when sleeping to help keep them in place in the moving water. Their nostrils and ears can close to keep out the water. Their dense fur creates a waterproof surface. Starfish can regrow their arms if they get bitten off or damaged. Shrimpfish protect themselves by swimming head downwards and pretending to be leaves. Some other examples of how aquatic lifeforms cope with water environments are:

Ducks have webbed feet to help them swim. (Some humans are born with webbed toes and fingers—around 1 in every 2,500 people).

Swans have long, muscular necks so that they can forage for food under the water's surface.

The Parrotfish makes a mucus bubble to sleep in—a kind of transparent sleeping bag that protects it from predators.

Archerfish spit at insects to knock them into the water where the fish can eat them.

The Water Boatman can walk on the meniscus (or the skin) of the water surface.

Male seahorses get pregnant and have babies (sometimes as many as 100 at a time).

The tiny Golfodulcean Poison Frog has enough toxin to kill 1,900 people.

Jellyfish are one of the oldest lifeforms on the planet, dating back to over 600 million years ago. They are related to sea anemones and coral.

Shark skin is so rough you can use it as sandpaper. If a shark stopped swimming, it would die, so it has to swim all the time. A swimming costume has been designed that copies sharkskin. It makes the wearer swim faster.

The octopus has powerful suckers on its eight legs and a hard beak, like a parrot. Its eyes can look in two separate directions and it has excellent vision. It squirts ink to confuse its predators. It has three hearts. It is very intelligent. Some aquariums give their resident octopuses puzzles such as Rubik cubes to keep them busy.

Ask the class to look up photographs of some of these creatures online or in books and make drawings of some of them.

Living with Water

If we could live underwater what would we do there?

In the past, some people, such as the Vikings, lived in places with a lot of water and were excellent sailors. They were living their lives half on water and half on land. The Bajau Laut people have lived almost entirely at sea for centuries. Floating markets and houses already exist. Could there be advantages to living with more water? Could we adapt to it? Could we swim to work and school, perhaps? Ask the class to find out about historical and contemporary people who have lived, or are living, closely with water. See Resources for Further Study for suggested books and websites.

Some architects, artists and designers are already working on ideas for how to live with more water in the future. Examples include floating cities that look like giant waterlilies (Vincent Callebaut) or an octopus, cities with robotic legs that can be raised up like stilts to move the entire city around and walk across the ocean floor (Ron Herron), an island created from plastic bottles netted together, boats made from an upturned table or hollowed out tree bark, a raft made from recycled plastic crates and barrels and white neoprene (the material used for wetsuits).

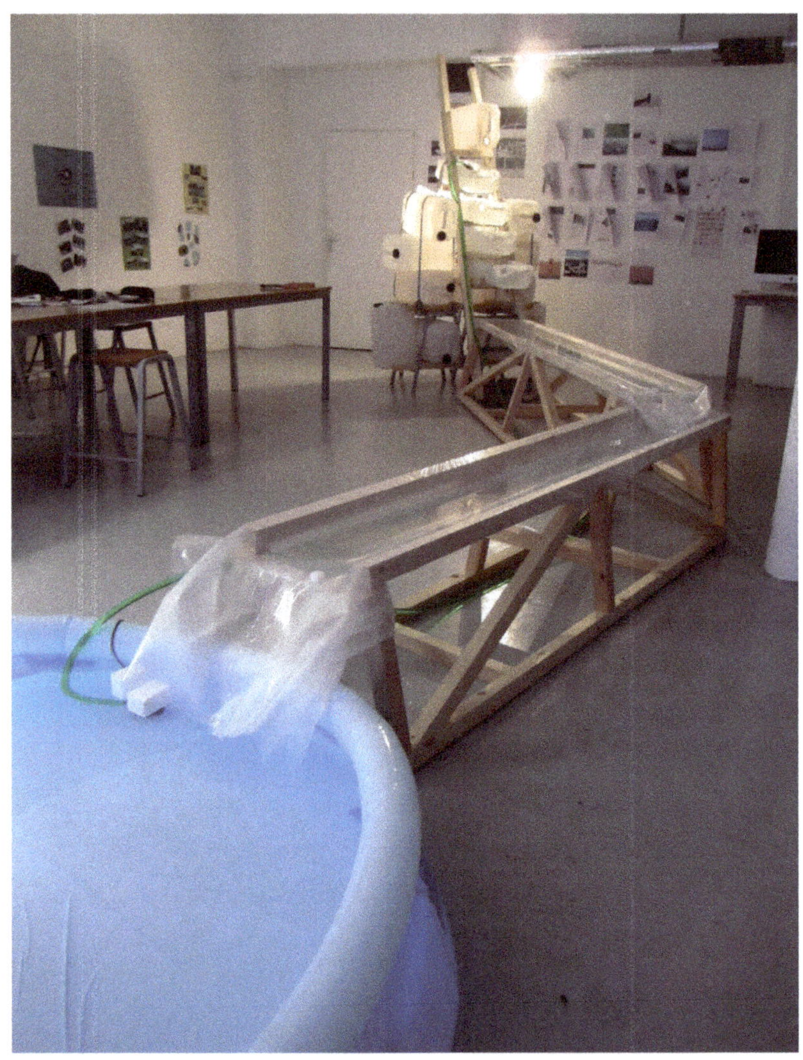

Urbonas Studio, Waterscape, *River Runs*, Modern Art
Oxford, UK, 2012. Photo by Nomeda Urbonas.

{ 3 }

Art Workshop

Water

Study water. Set up some experiments with the class to see how water behaves. Here are some examples:

Using a pipette or a straw, place a small drop of water on a clean surface. Does the water drop keep its shape?

Place two drops of water close to one another. Do they move towards each other? Water is slightly magnetically polarised so that it tends to seek out and try to reconnect with other water.

Fill a large fish tank or sink with water. Test out various materials to see what floats and what sinks. Use a straw to blow air across the surface of the water and to blow bubbles underwater. Use your hands to create waves and swirls in the water. Watch how the water behaves and then settles down.

Drop some other liquids such as ink, olive oil, washing up liquid, shampoo into the water and observe how the water behaves in response. (Children should check with an adult that they are using safe liquids.)

If you have access to hydrophones you can make some great sounds with water. Sound can travel four times faster in water than in air. When we are immersed in water we hear through our skulls rather than our ears.

Place a piece of tracing paper over a map and trace the shapes of rivers.

Put a drop of water at the top of an inclined surface and watch the shape of the path it makes on it downward, gravitational movement. Rivers never flow in straight lines, they wind and meander, and they split into smaller rivers that look like veins when they are near the sea.

Water is reflective, like a mirror and interacts with light. Set up an experiment to see this in action.

Waterscapes

Ask the class to discuss the various types of waterscapes they know about or have visited (e.g., islands, coasts, rivers, lakes, estuaries).

Working individually, ask the participants to sketch or make a water colour painting of a waterscape that they know, remember or imagine. It doesn't have to be real.

Working in small groups, ask them to lay out their sketches on the floor and see if they can organise them into one continuous landscape. What could be added? Working in a group, ask them to design a waterscape as outlined below.

Design and build a miniature waterscape in the classroom or outside. What could it be? What could it look like? What materials do you need? You could make a 2D or 3D model of a waterscape by painting, using textures, sewing, gluing, constructing. Whenever you are working with water, don't forget to have a mop, bucket and towels handy.

You can collect your own recycled materials to use and visit a recycling centre. Other materials can be found in art and craft shops (or through online suppliers). Aquarium supply shops and chandlers may also be sources of materials. You could go on a mudlarking journey and collect material from the water's edge to create a waterscape.

You could use fabric, collage and felt to create a large seascape or paint sea and islands on large sheets of paper.

A waterscape could be constructed using a paddling pool. You can make a waterfall and river by using an A-Frame step ladder (around 6 feet high), recycled large, plastic containers that can be cut in half to be strapped to the step ladder, plastic tie-fixers to attach the containers to the step-ladder, heavy-duty transparent sheets of plastic to hold the 'river', a wooden structure to support the 'river' in the plastic sheets that goes from the waterfall to the pool, an aquarium or pond water pump with tubing long enough to reach the water supply and to recycle the water around the landscape. (See the illustration on page 10.)

Or you could use a wooden half-barrel to make a pond using a pond-liner and a floating water aerator. Stock the pond with little fish to eat insects.

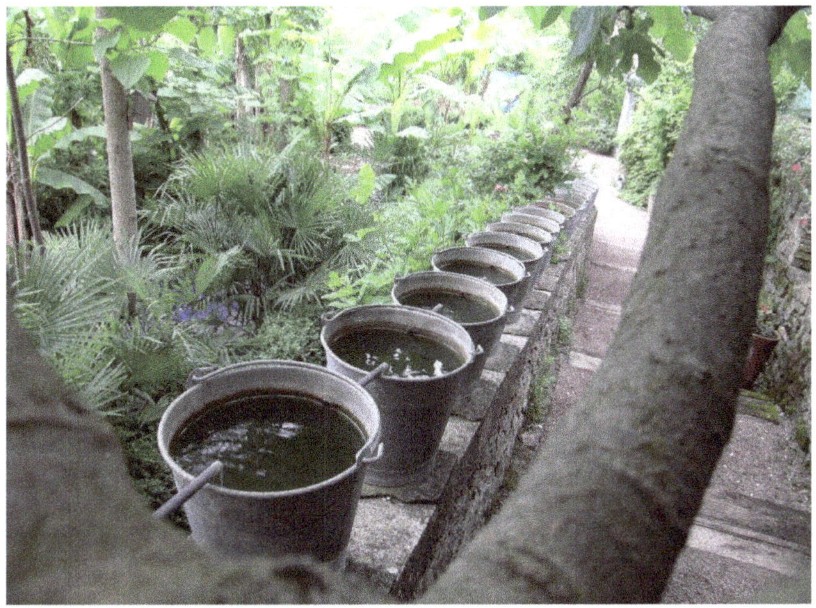

Jardin des Paradis, Cordes-sur-Ciel, France. Courtesy of Jardin des Paradis.

Or if you have a number of steps in a garden, you could place metal buckets with long spouts for the water to fall into the next bucket down and use a pump to keep it recycling. (See the illustration above.)

Aquatic Life

Study aquatic life. You could go to an aquarium, a natural history museum or a large aquarium supplies shop to find out more about lifeforms that live in water. Or you could go on a fieldtrip to a Wetlands Centre, or a coastal nature reserve. Look at books, magazines and websites on aquatic life. (There are some listed in Resources for Further Study.)

Ask each member of the class, to choose one type of aquatic life and create a mind-map diagram of all the ways that it is adapted to life in water.

Inventions for Living with Water

If there is a chandler's or a boating store near you, you could visit it to get some ideas about how to waterproof everyday things. You could visit a maritime or boating museum to get some ideas.

Present the workshop as follows:

Put white paper tablecloths on your desks and tape them down with masking tape so that they don't slip around.

Talk about how you might invent ways of living in, on or under water. Think about houses, boats, clothes, food, etc. Make drawings of your inventions on the tablecloths.

Make models of your inventions.

Materials to make models: acrylic paint—various colours for painting model inventions; A3 paper for drawing/painting inventions/mind maps; paint brushes, pots and mixing pallets; pencils/felt pens; glue guns (to be used with the help of an adult) and glue sticks; PVA glue; art knives (to be used with the help of an adult); scissors; old flipflops; small wood pieces; corks; recycled plastic bottles, pots and lolly sticks, and any other interesting floatable material; pipe cleaners; twigs; toy aquatic flora and fauna (you could buy a few things from an aquarium shop); coloured elastic bands; straws.

Test your model inventions on your waterscape if you have built one, or in a sink or large fish tank filled with water.

Using your inventions, you can make a film about living in your waterscape by using a mobile phone camera.

{ 4 }

Writing Workshop

Introduce the workshop as follows:

We are going to write a story together and learn some of the tricks of the trade of being a writer.

Put white paper tablecloths on your desks and tape them down with masking tape so that they don't slip around. Ask the group:

Do you have a favourite book?

Have you written some stories before that you are happy with?

Are some of you interested in being a writer as a job?

The story we are going to write together is about the future. At the end of the session we will make a sound recording of our story.

Most stories have a basic, similar structure:

1 There is a main character or characters

2 There is the world they are in—the time, the place, the situation, things around them, friends

3 They have a problem or challenge which means they have to leave home to solve the problem

4 They go on a journey encountering adventures and more problems

5 They return home and solve the problem.

THE END.

Getting Started

Divide into two (or more groups) of 3–6 people.

In the year 2516 planet Earth was all covered in water, and [?] and [?] lived in a city that floated on the sea. The city looked like a waterlily/an octopus/walked across the ocean floor on robotic legs.

[Complete the names. Select the city option. Use this as the beginning of the story.]

What are the names of the two main characters—a boy and a girl?

And what about this floating city they are living in—can we give it a bit more detail?

What are their houses like?

How do they get around, what do they wear? [sharkskin swimming costumes, otter fur coats, special boats?]

How do they get food and water? [vegetables growing on the sides and roofs of their houses, big fishing nets hanging off the city?]

What is the weather like?

Use your tablecloths to write down or draw a few ideas in pairs and then share the ideas.

The writer or teacher should note down the emerging story or stories throughout this process.

The Problem

There was a problem in the city.… What could the problem be?

[water, food, heat, vegetables dying or growing too much, no fish, too much plastic garbage, something else?]

Groups—Up and Down: Into Space or Underwater

Your characters set off to solve the problem. One character goes down into the depths of the ocean. The other character goes up into space towards other planets.

Develop the characters. Give them characteristics special to them. Think of your favourite characters in books. What special characteristics do they have? For example, Harry Potter has a lightning scar on his forehead and wears glasses.

What do your characters take with them on their journey? An object, a pet, a friend?

Describe the underwater or space setting.

What happens?

They are looking for a solution for the problem back home.

They return home and solve the problem.

Ending

End with a bang not a whimper.

The ending should be unexpected but believable.

An ending might return us to the beginning but with a changed situation.

An ending might be an image of continuing, for example, snow falling over everything, sun shining over everything, the sea rolling backwards and forwards.

Rewriting

During a break, the writer or teacher should tidy up the collated notes into a story or stories.

Now, tell the class:

Writing is 90% rewriting. Let's reconsider our story.

The teacher should read back the draft story to the group.

What are we aiming to say with our story? Can we make that stronger anywhere in the story?

We might want to weave the groups' stories around each other to make it into one story?

Can we make a more striking first sentence? A beginning has to grip the reader, plunge them straight into the story and make them curious to read on, for example:

'It was a bright cold day in April and the clocks were striking thirteen.' (George Orwell, Nineteen Eighty-Four*)*

Is our ending strong enough?

What is our title? It could be the name of a place or a character. Something that puts the story in a nutshell. Something that makes the reader focus on one aspect in particular.

Use your tablecloths to make a drawing for a book cover for the story with the story title.

Recording and Presenting

Divide the story up into sections to be read by each member of the group. Make a sound recording. The whole group can say the title of the story at the beginning. At the end say the name of the class or group together.

You could broadcast your story with a local radio station, present it as a sound file, or as a play.

You can also make an exhibition with your tablecloth drawings, and you can make photographs of your tablecloth drawings and notes.

You could make a book of your story or publish it online.

{ 5 }

Sample Story

The Mission for the Future

By the Year 5 Girls of Shaftoe Trust Primary School, Haydon Bridge, UK. The result of a future fiction workshop with writer, Tracey Warr.

Sanjay sighed. He was playing chess with the octopus and it was winning, as usual. Coral sat on a turtle-shell seat, sipping tea from a sea-shell cup, watching the chess game. Coral and Sanjay lived in the city of Lotus that floated on the sea and looked like a waterlily. The tsunami every Sunday generated energy for the city. In school, everybody learnt to sing the languages of the fish and sea animals, so that they could work together, helping each other. Everybody had a friendly seahorse or dolphin instead of the old-fashioned cars. When they needed to travel they sent a call out underwater.

Food grew up the sides of the houses and on the roofs. A vase machine filtered fresh water from salty water. Electric eels in tanks generated power for computers. Rubbish was collected by robot servants and fed to the sharks or dissolved harmlessly in the water. During the day, the moon and stars were shining, and the nights were usually sunny. In the daytime, whales swam around the city and light squirted out of their blow holes helping everyone to see. The sharks guarded the entrances to the city.

Coral got bored with the chess game and looked out of the window at a traffic warden octopus directing boats and swimmers around the floating fish and chip shop. In the park, the children were jumping on the sharkskin trampoline, swinging on the seaweed swing and whooping down the sand-slide. Houses rolled or floated upside down. A whale was waiting at the bus station with a carriage attached behind.

Coral stood up and went off to take a quick shower in a whale's blow hole. She cleaned her teeth with blue algae toothpaste that made her teeth very white. Afterwards a whale helped her brush her hair with his baleen mouth bristles. She put on her clothes made from fake sea otter fur to keep her warm and fake sharkskin to make her swim faster.

When Sanjay went swimming his long hair was swept up into his swim cap. He wore a breathing mask with electronic goggles that gave him information on everything he saw. If a fish swam past, his goggles told him which fish it was and if it was dangerous. His pet sea otter kept him company.

Sanjay and Coral waited as usual for the tsunami on Sunday that provided much of the energy for Lotus City. Everything was tightly tied down to cope with the weekly, huge, powerful wave. Twelve noon came but nothing happened. Sanjay looked at Coral with his eyebrows raised. 'What's happened? No tsunami!'

The worried murmurs amongst all the people grew louder and louder. They only had enough energy stored up for the next two weeks. After that everything would stop working and the city would start to sink.

And there was another problem! The sea was suddenly full of floating plastic bags. They were harming the fish and animals that lived and worked alongside the people of Lotus City.

Coral went down into the depths of the ocean to solve the problem of the plastic bags. She swallowed a tablet that allowed her to breathe underwater and took a dive off the city edge into the sea. The extra bone in Coral's ear allowed her to swim down deep. Her belt kept everything she needed strapped to her including her octopus ink squirter to scare off any attackers. The cape attached to her swimming costume kept her warm.

She found an animal stuck inside a plastic bag and freed it with her shark tooth necklace. Could this problem get worse? Using her computer monitor and DNA testing she was able to solve the problem. All the plastic used hundreds of years ago was kept in an enormous net tethered to the biggest iceberg at the South Pole. The net had been accidentally ripped by a passing water porcupine and plastic bags had started leaking out into the ocean. Coral repaired the ragged hole in the net.

Meanwhile Sanjay went up into space in a rocket towards other planets to solve the problem of the missing tsunami. He was heading for the sea planet, but a rock got caught in his engine and he crash landed on the moon. Why was the moon looking so dull? He realised it was covered in slime made by a visiting alien. 'Why are you doing this?' Sanjay asked.

The alien was from the planet of darkness and the moon was making things too bright there. Sanjay suggested they could move to a planet further away and the alien was happy to agree. Sanjay hoovered up the slime on the moon and solved the problem of the missing tsunami.

Coral and Sanjay met back at Lotus City with a sigh of relief and went together to a clown fish party.

Resources for Further Study

Some of the following books and websites may be of assistance to you.

Books for Children

(2015) *Ocean: A Children's Encyclopedia*, London: Dorling Kindersley.

Bailey, Jacqui (2004) *A Drop in the Ocean: The Story of Water*, London: A & C Black.

Byatt, Andrew; Fothergill, Alastair & Holmes, Martha (2001) *The Blue Planet: A Natural History of the Oceans*, London: BBC Worldwide.

CGP Books (2014) *KS2 Discover & Learn: History: Vikings Study Book, Year 5 & 6*, Broughton-in-Furness: Coordination Group Publications.

Defoe, Daniel (2007) *Robinson Crusoe* (Young Reading Series), London: Usborne.

Grahame, Kenneth (2012) *The Wind in the Willows* (Young Reading Series), London: Usborne.

Herman, Gail & WHO HQ (2018) *What Is Climate Change? (What Was?)*, New York: Random House.

Lee, Dora (2011) *Biomimicry: Inventions Inspired by Nature*, Toronto: Kids Can Press.

Madgewick, Wendy (2014) *Water Play: 18 Easy to Follow Experiments ... About Rain, Ice and How Water Works*, Helotes, Texas: Armadillo Books.

Olien, Rebecca (2016) *The Water Cycle at Work*, North Mankato, Minnesota: Capstone Press.

Ransome, Arthur (2012) *Swallows and Amazons*, London: Vintage Children's Classics.

Rose, Malcolm (2017) *Water Cycle*, London: Red Shed.

Stewart, Melissa (2014) *Water*, London: National Geographic Kids.

Books for Teachers

Ballard, J.G. (2014) *The Drowned World*, London: Fourth Estate.

Deakin, Roger (2000) *Waterlog*, London: Vintage.

Fishman, Charles (2011) *The Big Thirst: The Secret Life and Turbulent Future of Water*, New York: Free Press.

Gooley, Tristan (2017) *How to Read Water: Clues & Patterns from Puddles to the Sea*, London: Sceptre.

Itäranta, Emmi (2014) *Memory of Water*, London: Harper Voyager.

Warr, Tracey (2018) *The Water Age and Other Fictions*, London: Meanda Books.

Websites

Bajau Laut Sea Nomads

jamesmorgan.co.uk/features/bajau-laut-sea-nomads

Predictive Flood Maps flood.firetree.net

Ron Herron, *Walking City on the Ocean*
www.moma.org/collection/works/814

Sea Life https://www.visitsealife.com

Urbonas Studio, *River Runs* www.vilma.cc/river

Vincent Callebaut, *Lilypads*
vin-
cent.callebaut.org/object/080523_lilypad/lilypad/projects/user

Wildfowl & Wetlands Trust www.wwt.org.uk

Thanks

A huge thank you to the children who participated in the River Runs Workshop at Modern Art Oxford, UK; The Water Age Art Workshop at Annantalo Art School, Helsinki, Finland; and The Water Age Writing Workshop at Shaftoe Trust School in Haydon Bridge, UK. These three events were the basis for this book and the exhilarating imaginations of those participants were the impetus for creating this book for others to engage with similar ideas and activities.

This book is based on workshops and research I undertook as an invited artist and writer in the following art projects: Urbonas Studio, *River Runs* at Modern Art Oxford, UK, 2012; *Frontiers in Retreat*, 2014-2018 (frontiersinretreat.org) with Jutempus, Lithuania; HIAP, Finland and the Centre d'Art i Natura, Catalonia/Spain; *Exoplanet Lot* with MAGCP (Maison des Arts Georges et Claude Pompidou, Cajarc), 2016 (www.magcp.fr/project/cet-ete-exoplanete-lot-parcours-dart-contemporain-en-vallee-du-lot03-07-04-09-2016); and Allenheads Contemporary Arts' *As Above So Below*, 2016 (www.acart.org.uk/as-above-so-below).

In addition to the workshop participants, many other people made significant contributions to the workshops' design or organisation. I am especially grateful to Julie Turley, who designed the first aquatic life workshops for children in *River Runs* at Modern Art Oxford. Many thanks to Tim Eastop at the Canal & River Trust and to Russell Robson at the Environment Agency for their enthusiastic support for *River Runs*. And thanks to my collaborators in *River Runs*: Nomeda and Gediminas Urbonas, and Giacomo Castagnola, and to all the participants in that project. Laura Degenhardt did a terrific job as Project Assistant.

Thank you to the participants in the Aquatic Biomimicry Workshop that I organised for OVADA in Oxford and especially Adrian Pawley, and thanks to those who joined us for *Future Rivers* in Oxford, and for the Learning from the River Workshop at MIT, which I led with Gediminas Urbonas.

I undertook residencies with Jutempus in Lithuania, US and Iceland; HIAP in Finland; and Centre d'Art i Natura in Catalonia/Spain in the *Frontiers in Retreat* project. I am grateful to Jenni Nurmenniemi at HIAP and Elsa Hessle (then the collaborating art teacher at Annantalo Art School) for their support with The Water Age Art Workshop. And thanks to Jaana Eskola, Salla Lahtinen, Lluis Llobet, Taru Elfving and all the other members of the *Frontiers in Retreat* network who provided various and valuable responses and inspirations at many points.

Thank you to La Source Zen café on the GR36 path, alongside the River Lot, near Saint Cirq Lapopie, and Carlos and Christine Hopps for assistance with the barrel pond in *Exoplanet Lot*. Thanks to the *Exoplanet Lot* curators, Martine Michard, Rob La Frenais and Ludwig, and my fellow artists in that residency and exhibition: Tania Candiani, HeHe, Thomas Lasbouygues, Caroline Le Méhauté and Ludwig.

Thanks to Helen Ratcliffe and Alan Smith at Allenheads Contemporary Arts and Shaftoe Trust Primary School for inviting me to run the writing workshop at Shaftoe Trust School in *As Above So Below*, 2016, which resulted in such a wonderful story. Thank you to the North Pennines Area of Outstanding Natural Beauty for funding that workshop.

Thank you to Jardin des Paradis, Nomeda Urbonas, James A. Hudson and Sergio Urbina for permission to use their photographs. And, finally, I am extremely grateful to James A. Hudson for his beautiful work on the book covers for The Water Age series.

ABOUT THE AUTHOR

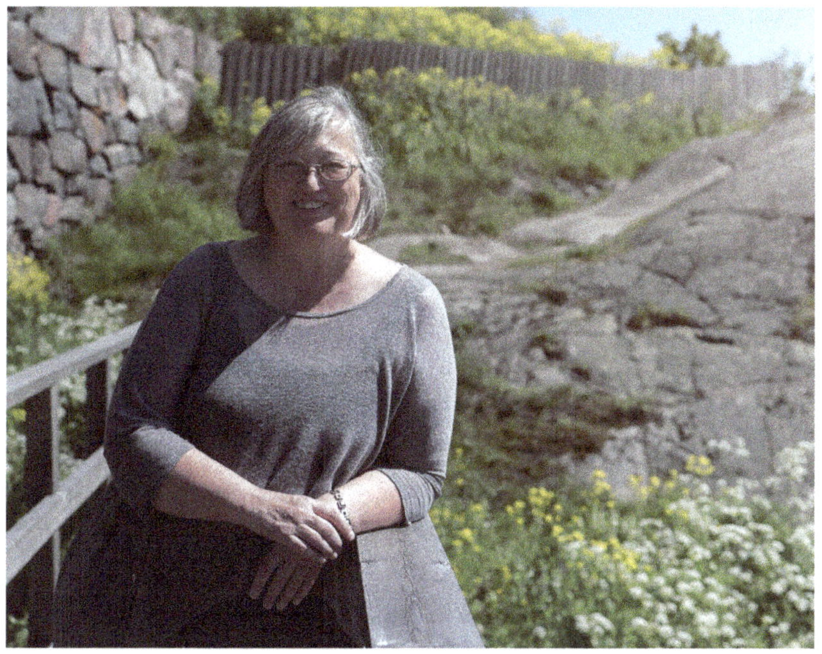

Tracey Warr. Photo by Sergio Urbina.

Tracey Warr is a fiction and non-fiction writer based in France. She describes herself as writing in the vicinity of art. She is an avid swimmer.

Tracey Warr's historical novels, set in France, England and Wales, are published by Meanda Books: *Almodis the Peaceweaver* (2011), *The Viking Hostage* (2014), *Conquest I: Daughter of the Last King* (2016), *Conquest II: The Drowned Court* (2017) and *Conquest III: The Anarchy* (2020). Her fiction has received awards from Literature Wales and Santander and was shortlisted for the Impress Prize.

Her published work on contemporary art includes *The Artist's Body* (Phaidon, 2000), *Remote Performances in Nature and Architecture* (Routledge, 2015) and *The Midden* (Garret, 2018). She has published numerous essays on contemporary artists with publishers including Intellect, Tate, Merrell/Barbican, Black Dog and Manchester University Press. She was an invited artist in the *Exoplanet Lot* exhibition and the *Frontiers in Retreat* five-year art and ecology research project.

She is working on a biography entitled *Three Female Lords,* about three sisters who lived in southern France and northern Spain in the 11th century. The biography has been supported by an Authors' Foundation Award.

She was Head of Dartington Arts School and established MA Poetics of Imagination there with Martin Shaw. She was Senior Lecturer in art history and theory at Oxford Brookes University and Dartington College of Arts in the UK. She was Guest Professor at Bauhaus University, Weimar, Germany; MIT, Cambridge, US; and

Piet Zwart Institute, Rotterdam, Netherlands. She is Course Leader in Art History at Saint Francis University Study Abroad Programme in France. She has led many creative writing and art writing courses and workshops.

https://meandabooks.com
https://traceywarrwriting.com
www.facebook.com/traceywarrARTwriting
www.facebook.com/traceywarrhistoricalwriting
@TraceyWarr1